The Origins of the Roman Rite

Volume 2

Gordon P Jeanes

Vicar of St Anne's Church, Wandsworth

Diocese of Southwark in the Church of England

GW00472343

GROVE BOOKS LIMITED

RIDLEY HALL RD CAMBRIDGE CB3 9HU

1

Contents

The Cover Illustration is a photo of the paschal candle-stand and ambo in the *titulus*
of St Lawrence outside the Walls. Photograph: author.
(*Titulus* was a term originally applied to the early 'house churches' of pre-Constantinian
Christian Rome, and later to the churches in an immediately around the city).

Abbreviations and works commonly used

Andrieu	M Andrieu, (ed.), *Les Ordines Romani du Haut Moyen Age*, 5 vols (Louvain, 1948-61).
CAP	A G Martimort, *the Church at Prayer* (ET 4 vols, Geoffrey Chapman, London, 1986-7).
DBL	E C Whitaker, *Documents of the Baptismal Liturgy* (2nd edn, SPCK, London, 1970).
ORR 1	G P Jeanes, *Origins of the Roman Rite*, vol. 1 (Alcuin/GROW Liturgical Study 20, Bramcote, 1991).
PL	Migne, *Patrologia Latina*.

Sacramentaries

Gelasian	ed. L C Mohlberg OSB, *Liber Sacramentorum Romanae Ecclesiae Ordinis Anni Circuli (Sacramentarium Gelasianum)* Rerum Ecclesisticarum Documenta, Series Maior, Fontes IV (Rome 1960).
Gregorian	ed. J Dehusses, *Le Sacramentaire Grégorien* (Editions Universitaires, Fribourg, Switzerland, 1971).

Note on the Translation

Sacerdos, often translated into English as 'priest', in the documents of this time was used for a bishop or for a presbyter without distinction, and whenever 'priest' occurs it has this meaning. Sometimes the word is rendered in more neutral terms such as 'sacred minister'. 'Presbyter' is translated as 'presbyter'.

In the translations of historic texts I despair of massaging away gender exclusion, anti-semitism etc. and normally reproduce the text without seeking to justify it.

Bibliographies

Bibliographies are kept to a minimum and are to be read alongside those in other standard text books.

Copyright © Gordon P Jeanes 1998

First Impression December 1998
ISSN 0951-2667
ISBN 1 85174 391 X

Introduction

In my former work (O Colin) I set out to reproduce as many of the central texts as I could manage along with illustrative material from various sources. I trust that it was a useful exercise, and perhaps the request to produce a second volume suggests it sold reasonably well. But I have decided to take a different approach in this volume, and translate a smaller number of texts more fully over a few narrow themes. Each of the three chapters has its own particular bent.

The first, on the liturgy of Holy Week and Easter, looks at the development of these liturgies from the fourth to the early ninth centuries, and also functions as a working example of how the liturgy of Rome interacted with that of her neighbours in that period. It is easy for the student to have a picture of Rome on one side, and Gaul on the other, with the former's liturgical practice pervading the latter's, first informally (Gelasian sacramentaries etc.) and then formally with Charlemagne's official adoption of the totally inappropriate Gregorian Sacramentary, which was rescued by the addition of a large appendix of Gallican material. The case of Holy Week and the Easter vigil, with the influence of Rome spreading wide, but also the influences on Rome of north Italy, and, more distantly, Byzantium and Jerusalem, give some useful shades of grey. I have not included all the points of influence in the commentary, but hopefully the translations will help students follow other scholarly discussions of the texts.

The second chapter gives the sections on Penance from the Gelasian Sacramentary. This topic is a focus of interest at present in the Church of England, but the basic material and indeed the whole logic of the ancient penitential system is not widely known, and so here I am trying simply to give some familiarity of the subject. Again I have not attempted a full commentary, but offer the text to be read together with the literature on the subject.

The third chapter returns to the subject of Rome and her neighbours, with a fairly full translation of a set of baptismal commentaries by a writer known until recently as Pseudo Maximus of Turin. I have three reasons for producing here what is not, strictly speaking, a Roman text. First, it is influential on our perception of Roman use because it has material in it which underlies the famous description of the baptismal liturgy by John the Deacon. Thus it reveals the subtle influence of non-Roman sources not on the liturgy itself but on its reception. Secondly it is an interesting text in itself and deserves to be better known in the English world, especially now that it has been published in a critical edition. Thirdly, to fly a personal kite, I believe that it contains earlier material, and have set out a summary of the evidence as the initial approach to a study I hope to engage in, looking at the whole genre of baptismal commentaries and how they relate to one another. Forgive me if you feel I have hijacked the volume in order to fly a private kite.

So this is a varied collection of material, but I hope that it will have something for everyone.

1
Rome and Her Neighbours:
Holy Week and the Paschal Vigil

As well as being interesting as a source of modern liturgical celebrations of Easter, the vigil service is a good example of many of the features of the early Roman rite. First, the extreme conservatism of the Papal liturgy which resisted for many years later popular developments which were adopted elsewhere in Italy and even allowed by Popes in other churches under their control. As a result, we have the variety between the Papal liturgy and that in the other churches, which historically lies behind the two families of sacramentaries (the celebrant's book), the Gelasian sacramentaries which originated in the parishes and dioceses around Rome, and the Gregorian sacramentary which was the Pope's own book. Thirdly, many of the documents reveal the intense interest outside Rome in its liturgy, leading to widespread imitation and application to local situations. Fourthly we see instances of early creativity and variety, particularly in the Easter proclamation which was a form of blessing of the paschal candle which was eventually reduced to a single form, the *Exultet*. (The custom of the Proclamation seems to have originated in north Italy.) Likewise there seems originally to have been considerable variety in the number and selection of vigil readings. Finally, the influence of non-Roman centres is important, particularly in the origin and spread of the proclamation, so that a feature which is now associated with the Roman liturgy was originally foreign to it and for many years resisted by the Papal liturgy.

BIBLIOGRAPHY
As well as general studies, recent works include:
G P Jeanes, *The Day has Come! Easter and Baptism in Zeno of Verona* (Alcuin Club Collection 73, Liturgical Press, Collegeville, Minnesota, 1995).
A J MacGregor, *Fire and Light in the Western Triduum* (Alcuin Club Collection 71, Liturgical Press, Collegeville, Minnesota, 1992).

To begin with the Papal liturgy, we have a large number of *Ordines* which deal with Holy Week and Easter. *Ordo 23* is a comparatively early one which dates from perhaps the first half of the eighth century. It was written, according to Andrieu, by a Frankish visitor to Rome who notes the particular interesting features of the Papal liturgy, but omits the mass of detail which afflicts such documents as *Ordo 1* which was designed to give clear directions to the participants. *Ordo 23* is descriptive rather than prescriptive.

Text: Andrieu

ORDO XXIII

[On the sacred triduum before Easter]

On the Thursday at matins they do not say, 'Lord open my lips', or the invitatory, or the 'Glory' to the psalm, or 'But you O Lord', or the prayer, or the litany 'Kyrie eleison', but only 'Christ became obedient for us'.

Then at mass around the seventh hour the Pope comes out from the Lateran palace and down through St John's basilica to the sacristy with the deacons and subdeacons in chasubles going before him to the sacristy. After they come out of the sacristy, the subdeacons go first in white albs and the deacons in dalmatics, and seven acolytes go before the lord Pope with seven candlesticks.

After 'Kyrie eleison', the lord Pope says, 'Glory to God in the highest', and everything happens in the same ways as on other festivals, except for 'Alleluia' and the chrism which is blessed on that day.

When he says, 'The peace of the Lord be always with you', he breaks one host in two pieces and he gives it to the archdeacon who places it on the paten which is held by a minister.

The archdeacon shares the other hosts among the presbyters and then he and all the presbyters break them. When the fraction is completed, the Pope alone makes his communion and then he blesses the chrism and, either himself or through the oblationary or [the text is corrupt], commands it to be taken to the *tituli* and the other churches.

Likewise and they make their communion from the holy sacrifice which they keep on the Friday and they go to their homes.

On the Friday, around the eighth hour, the lord Pope comes down from the Lateran palace to St John's basilica, but both he and the other ministers of the holy church are barefooted, and they come before the altar.

And the lord Pope orders the light to be brought from the large lamp[1], and the light is brought from it by two white tapers which he has ordered to be carried by two clergy of the household before the lord.

They process out of St John's to the psalm, 'Blessed are they whose way of life is blameless', [Ps 118 (119)] with the archdeacon holding the left hand of the lord Pope and the bishop himself carrying in his right hand a thurible with incense, and another deacon behind the lord Pope carrying the wood of the precious Cross in a golden reliquary adorned with jewels. The Cross itself of precious wood is covered with gold and jewels; inside it has a hollow arrangement for balsam with a beautiful fragrance.

---

1 *Ungiarius*: this seems to have been a large oil lamp which, as one of three, was kept lit from the Thursday to Easter Day. Pope Zacharias describes the custom (*Ep 13 to Boniface*, PL 89, 951): 'On the Thursday of Holy Week, when the holy chrism is consecrated, three large lamps, holding oil which is collected from the various lamps in the church, burn in a hidden part of the church continually through the period in the likeness of the inner tabernacle (of Holy Sepulchre in Jerusalem), and great care is taken, so that the oil will be sufficient to keep the lamp burning to the third day. On Holy Saturday the new fire is taken from these lamps by the sacred ministers for the baptism at the sacred font.'

When they come to the church of Holy Cross in Jerusalem, they enter the church and the deacon places the reliquary containing the Cross on the altar and straightway the lord Pope opens it.

Then he prostrates himself before the altar in prayer, then rises, kisses the Cross, and goes and stands at the chair. At his bidding the bishops, priests, deacons and subdeacons kiss the Cross on the altar. Then it is placed on a stand at the sanctuary gates and there the rest of the congregation kisses it. However the women do not enter there, but afterwards the oblationary and other subdeacons take it to be kissed by the women.

But when the Cross has been kissed by the lord Pope, at once a subdeacon goes up into the ambo and begins to read the reading of the prophet Hosea, and after he has come down a cantor goes up and sings the gradual, 'Lord I have heard' [Habakkuk 3.2.] with its verses.

The subdeacon goes up again and reads the second reading, of Deuteronomy, and after him the cantor goes up and begins the tract 'Whoever dwells' [Ps 90 (91)]. When this is completed, a barefooted deacon goes with the gospel, accompanied by two subdeacons, and reads the passion of the Lord according to John.

When the gospel has been read, the lord Pope says the prayer, 'Let us pray for the holy Church of God', and the archdeacon says, 'Let us bend the knee', and afterwards, 'Arise', and the rest in its order, and at the end he simply says, 'The Lord be with you', and they reply, 'And with your spirit'.

And they process again to the Lateran, to the psalm 'Blessed are they whose way of life is blameless'.

However the Pope does not make his communion there, nor the deacons. Anyone who wishes to receive communion does so from the sacrament reserved from the sacrifice which was kept on the Thursday. And anyone who does not wish to receive communion there goes to the other churches of Rome or to the *tituli* and receives communion there.[1]

On Holy Saturday, about the seventh hour, the clergy enter the church, for the lord Pope does not. And they go to the sacristy, that is the deacons and the subdeacons in their chasubles and the two regionary notaries light tapers one each from the same light which is hidden from Friday,[2] and they come to the altar. The deacons stand at the chair and the bishops sit in the choir. A reader

---

1   Communion from the reserved sacrament on Good Friday as a public rite (different from the domestic custom of former times) is practised in the *tituli*, the churches of the city, but not at the Papal service. In effect it is provided for, but as a private devotion afterwards.

2   The service is led by the deacons, but does not include the blessing of the paschal candle. The two candles mentioned here are a distinctive feature of the Roman rite of the vigil, and whatever their origin (quite possibly in the ancient *lucernarium* rites) they were now each the size of an adult and seem to have been taken to represent the two angels at the tomb of Christ. See *Fire and Light*, pp 431-9.

goes up into the ambo and reads a reading in Greek.[1] There follows 'In the beginning'. and the prayers and 'Let us bow the knee' and the tract.

When this is complete, they go down to the baptistery and the choir sings the litany three times: 'Christ hear us' and the rest.

Afterwards the lord Pope blesses the font and when he comes to the place when he says, 'May the power of your Holy Spirit descend into all the water of this font',[2] the regionary notaries put the tapers which they are holding into the font.

When he has finished the blessing he sprinkles water on the people and begins the baptisms.

After he has baptized four or five infants, he goes out and the presbyters and two deacons do the baptisms, and he then seals the candidates and anoints them with chrism.

Afterwards the choir sings two litanies and at the third they enter into the mass—it is now late—and he says 'Glory to God in the highest' and 'Alleluia, Give thanks to the Lord', [Ps 117 (118)] and the tract 'Bless the Lord'.

And the choir sings 'Lamb of God' and four acolytes reply who are standing at the sanctuary gates holding bowls and vessels which afterwards they hold for the communion of the people.

The Vigil Service in the Papal Liturgy

The above *Ordo* gives only the briefest reference to the conduct of the vigil service. But we have fuller details in a manuscript given by Andrieu as the appendix to *Ordo 28*. It is very similar to the one summarized above, even retaining the inclusion of the readings in Greek as well as Latin. Then we have the prayers said by the Pope as set out in the Gregorian Sacramentary. One reading is different but otherwise the same liturgy is being described.

Much of the literature on the vigil readings presupposes that originally the vigil was composed of twelve readings, and that the five in the Papal tradition was a later reduction. However in my study of Zeno of Verona I have identified there a custom of five readings in the later fourth century, and suggest that it is at least as ancient as that of twelve.[3]

---

1 The custom of having the readings in Greek as well as Latin dates from the period of Byzantine occupation of Rome in the sixth century. It does not survive into the later sacramentaries.
2 The blessing of the font is given by Whitaker, *DBL*, p187. For dipping the tapers into the font. see *Fire and Light*, pp 476-7.
3 *The Day has Come!*, pp 200-20.

Text: Andrieu

Appendix to ORDO XXVIII
Here begins about Holy Saturday

The bishop and the others dress as on ordinary days. Two large candles precede him, and he goes up to the altar and prays there in silence. From there he goes up to the chair and sits down.

A subdeacon at once removes his chasuble, goes up in the ambo and when he reads he does not say, 'A reading from the book Genesis', but begins thus: 'In the beginning God made heaven and earth'. All the other readings are begun in this way. First it is read in Greek, then immediately by another person in Latin.

Then the bishop first rises and says, 'Let us pray'. The deacon says, 'Let us bow the knee', then, 'Arise'. And the bishop says the prayer.

And the reading, 'And it happened in the morning watch' [Exodus 14.24] is read in Greek and this canticle is sung by the same person in Greek, 'Let us sing to the Lord' [Exodus 15.1]. After this another one goes up and reads the above reading in Latin and sings the above canticle in Latin.

Then the bishop rises and say, 'Let us pray', and the deacon does as before, and the prayer is said.

After this the reading 'Seven women shall take hold of one man' [Isaiah 4.1.] is read in Greek and the same person sings the canticle 'The vine' [Isaiah 5.1.] in Greek. Then another goes up to read the above in Latin and sings the above canticle in Latin.

And the bishop, 'Let us pray', the deacon as above.

And again the reading 'Moses wrote a song' [Deuteronomy 31.22.] is read in Greek. And another goes up and reads it in Latin.

Then the bishop and deacon as above.

After this is sung the psalm, 'As the hart desires' [Ps. 41 (42)] in Greek, and another sings the same psalm in Latin.

After this the bishop turns to the people and says, 'The Lord be with you'. They respond, 'And with your spirit'. And he says 'Let us pray', and turns east to say the prayer. When it is finished he says, 'The Lord be with you', and at once goes down to the baptistery.

The Gregorian Sacramentary: Paschal Vigil
PRAYERS WHICH ARE SAID FOR THE READINGS IN CHURCH
Reading of the book Genesis: In the beginning God made heaven and earth. [Genesis 1.1]

O God, you marvellously created humanity and more marvellously redeemed us, grant us, we beseech you, that we may stand firm against the pleasures of sin with a firm mind, so that we may be worthy to come to eternal joys. Through our Lord . . .

Reading of the book Exodus: And it happened in the morning watch. [Exodus 14.24]

God, we see the sparkle of your ancient miracles even in this present age. Grant, we pray, that even as you freed your first people from the Egyptians, you may work the same for the salvation of the nations through the waters of baptism. Through . . .

Reading of the prophet Isaiah: And seven women shall take hold of one man. [Isaiah 4.1]

O God, you bid us in the pages of both testaments to celebrate the paschal mystery, grant us to understand your mercy, so that from the reception of present gifts we may have a firm expectation of gifts to come. Through our Lord . . .

Reading of the prophet Isaiah: This is the inheritance for those who believe in the Lord. [Isaiah 57.17]

O God, you continually enlarge your Church by calling the nations; mercifully grant that you may protect with your continual protection those whom you wash in the water of baptism. Through our Lord.

Concerning psalm 41: As the hart desires

Grant, we beseech you, almighty God, that we who celebrate the paschal feast with the fire of heavenly desires may thirst for the fountain of life. Through our Lord.

Another prayer at the same psalm 41: Almighty and everlasting God, graciously look on the devotion of your new born people who like the hart seek the fountain of your water, and graciously grant that the thirst of that faith may sanctify body and soul by the mystery of baptism. Through our Lord.

Imitation of the Papal Liturgy outside Rome

Ordo Romanus 24 is a document which illustrates the close imitation of the Papal liturgy in a neighbouring city. Andrieu locates its setting in one of the 'suburbicarian' dioceses, that is, the cities of central and southern Italy which were immediately subject to Rome's authority. The imitation is so close as to be almost artificial: not only do we have mention of the bishop who is the main celebrant but also other attendant bishops (like the bishops of the suburban dioceses of Rome). Various clergy bear the titles of their Roman counterparts, and the practice of holding the services in different churches around the city is followed. In smaller cities these arrangements must have presented practical difficulties. But there are also differences from the Papal liturgy. Communion from the reserved sacrament on Good Friday is a public liturgy, with a form of consecration of the chalice using the consecrated bread reserved from the previous day. Other details which will be mentioned in the footnotes reveal that the sacramentary used was closer to the Gelasian family than to the Papal Gregorian book.

Text: Andrieu

ORDO XXIV

[On the services from the Wednesday of the great week up to Easter]

On the Wednesday which is the day before the Lord's Supper, at the third hour, the bishop comes to the altar in the major church with his clergy as usual and says the solemn prayers in this manner: 'Let us pray', and he says the prayer, 'O God from whom Judas received the punishment of his guilt'. Afterwards follows 'Amen' and he says the solemn prayers as they are found in the Sacramentary, only he omits the prayer for himself. After the emperor he says a prayer for the king of the Franks, then the rest in order. At the last prayer, for the Jews, they do not bend the knee.[1] When they are finished, he kisses the altar and leaves.

Afterwards, at the eighth hour, they go into the mass in this order: The choir says the antiphonary for the introit, he says the prayer. One reading is read as it is noted in the Capitulary.[2] There follows the gradual responsory, 'Do not turn your face' [Ps 68 (69)] Another reading follows, and after it the canticle, 'Lord, hear' [Ps 101 (102)] with its five verses. The gospel is announced by the deacon thus: 'The passion of our Lord Jesus Christ according to Luke'. When it has been read, the mass is celebrated as usual.

On the Thursday, the Lord's Supper, at the third hour, the bishop and all the deacons enter the sacristy and put on dalmatics and all their finery, and the bishop sits in his chair.

Two vases of oil are prepared. The better one is taken to the bishop, who is given balsam and mixes it with the oil and with his own hand he fills the vase. The ministers keep the other which is already full. The bishop washes his hands and processes with seven candlesticks to the mass. When the antiphon has been said for the introit, he says the prayer.

The reading from the apostle is read, 'Brethren, when you come together' up to 'that we may not be condemned with this world' [1 Cor. 11.20-32]. The gradual responsory follows, 'Christ was humbled for us' [Phil. 2. 8-9].

The Gospel according to John is read, chapter 112, 'At that time, Jesus, knowing that his hour had come' up to 'as I have done for you, so you must do for one another'. [John 13.1-15] And straightway the mass is celebrated as usual. When it is completed, only the bishop receives communion and the deacon administers him the chalice, only on that day. After he has received communion, he places the chalice on the altar; then he receives the paten from the subdeacon and places it next to the chalice on the left side, and at once it is covered by two deacons with a clean cloth . . . [details of the preparation of the oil are omitted here] Then the bishop looks towards the east and the deacon holds the vase of oil

---

1 Pure antisemitism.
2 The Capitulary was a lectionary in the sense of providing a list of readings but not their full text.

before him in his left arm with the veil pulled back, as we have specified above. And the bishop says, 'Lift up your hearts' Response: 'We have them with the Lord'. And he proceeds with the consecration of the chrism in a loud voice. But before it is blessed, he blows on it and breathes three times into the vase.

When this is finished, he blesses the vase of oil in the manner set out above. He breathes on it in the same way three times, but quietly.

But the vase of chrism, the moment it has been blessed, is covered and may be seen by no one. But an acolyte holds it and everyone reverences it in their ranks.

When this is finished, the bishop washes his hands and comes before the altar and the whole people receive communion in the usual manner.

On the Friday at the third hour, all the presbyters both from the city and the suburban churches and all the clergy with the people come together in a particular church within the city, though not in the major church, to wait for the bishop or one who will take his place. When he comes out of the sacristy he processes before the altar to pray in the order which is found in the Sacramentary.[1] As soon as he has got up he goes up in silence to the chair. When he has sat down, at once a subdeacon does up to read the lesson, and after the lesson is sung the canticle, Lord I have heard' [Habakkuk 3] with its verses. Then follows the second lesson, and after it follows the tract, 'Whoever dwells in the defence' [Ps. 90 (91)] or 'Deliver me, O Lord' [Ps. 139 (140)].

When this is finished, the passion of our Lord according to John is read. Afterwards the bishop comes before the altar and says: 'Let us prayer'; Deacon: 'Let us bend the knee; Arise, Let us pray, dearly beloved, first for the holy church of God', as we have said above for the Wednesday.

When he has finished them, at once two deacons strip off the altar the cloth which formerly had been under the gospel book. And thus all go out in silence.

But the presbyters of the churches, both those of the city and suburban churches, go to the churches to celebrate vespers in this manner, with only one

---

1 This preliminary prayer is found in the Gelasian but not the Gregorian sacramentary. The Gelasian directs the proceedings thus:

XLI

THE BEGINNING OF THE ORDER FOR FRIDAY OF THE LORD'S PASSION

At the ninth hour they all process to the church, and the holy cross is placed on the altar. The bishop comes out of the sacristy in silence without any singing, and they come before the altar. The bishop asks the congregation to pray for him and says, Let us pray, and the deacon announces, Let us bend the knee. And after a little while he says, Arise, and the bishop says the prayer.

O God, from whom Judas received the punishment of his guilt and the thief the reward of his confession, grant us the effect of your propitiation so that just as Christ our Lord gave recompense to each according to their merits, so he may remove our old sins and bestow upon us the grace of his resurrection. Who lives with you.

When the prayer is finished he goes behind the altar and the reading is read . . .

(For the following part of the service see *ORR 1*, p 32)

difference, that, where the bishop makes mention of the Pope, they name their bishop.

At evening, both in the church in which the bishop says the prayers and in the other churches of the presbyters, after the prayers a cross is prepared behind the altar, with a space between it and the altar, and it is carried out from here by two acolytes.

A faldstool is placed before it, and the bishop comes and kisses the cross in adoration, then the other bishops, presbyters, deacons and other clergy according to their rank, then the people.

The bishop returns to the chair while everyone is reverencing the cross.

Two presbyters, who are among the first to have reverenced it, immediately enter the sacristy or wherever is placed the Body of the Lord which was reserved from the previous day. They place it on a paten and a subdeacon takes before them a chalice of unconsecrated wine, and another subdeacon the paten with the Body of the Lord.

As they take it, one presbyter takes the paten and the other, the chalice, and they place them on the bare altar.

The bishop remains seated while the people venerate the cross.

For, during the veneration of the cross by the bishop or people, the antiphon is continually sung: 'Behold the wood of the cross on which the salvation of the world hung. Come, let us adore'. Psalm 118 (119) is said.

When the cross has been venerated and put back in its place, the bishop comes down behind the altar and says, 'Let us pray, as we are commanded for our salvation, Our Father'. There follows, 'Deliver us, we beseech you, Lord'.

When they have said 'Amen', he takes a piece of the consecrated bread and places it in the chalice, without saying anything.[1] And all receive communion in silence and everything is concluded. 'In the name of the Father and of the Son and of the Holy Spirit. Peace be to you'. Response: 'And with your spirit'. End.

From the evening of the Thursday to the Saturday morning the altars are bare and on the Thursday the response is not sung at vespers.

On Holy Saturday, all come to the church. At that point two candles are lit, held by two notaries, one at the right corner of the altar and the other at the left.[2]

A reader goes up into the ambo. He does not announce 'A reading from the book Genesis', but begins simply, 'In the beginning'. Likewise with the other

---

[1]   This action of placing the consecrated bread in the chalice effects the consecration of the wine. Communion is thus in both kinds. Cf. *ORR1*, p 45, note 2, and *CAP* vol. 3, 111f. P. Nautin, 'Le Rite du "Fermentum" dans les Eglises Urbaines de Rome' in *Ephemerides Liturgicae* 96 (1982), pp 510-22. This fully developed liturgy is very different from what we saw in the Papal mass.

[2]   The twin candles follows closely the Roman custom described above. There is no mention of a blessing of a paschal candle.

readings. And they do not say a prayer before 'In the beginning'.[1]

When the readings are finished, at once one minister comes, holding vases [of the oil] in his hands, and stands at the right corner of the altar. Then he goes up, leading the bishop, to the baptistery.

Then the choir goes down to the baptistery to sing the litany, waiting ready for the bishop.

The succentor holds in his left hand, through the chasuble, the golden vessel from which the bishop pours chrism into the font, and when they are ordered they sing the third litany.

Then the bishop processes with all state, supported by two deacons. The two candlesticks which had been previously lit, always process before him to the end of the service.

As soon as he has come to the baptistery, he stands and blesses the fonts according to custom by memory.[2] He makes the first cross at 'Let thy Holy Spirit . . . give fecundity to this water', dividing the water with his hand in the form of a cross; the second at 'Wherefore I bless you'; likewise the third at 'I bless you also through Jesus Christ'.[3]

When the font has been blessed, he pours in chrism with the golden vessel and sprinkles the water over the people with his hand.

Then he baptizes and returns to the sacristy. He waits until the infants have been clothed, when he confirms them. Then the choir is bidden to sing the litany before the altar, first one sevenfold, then after a gap another one fivefold, then again after a gap threefold.

And when he says, 'Lamb of God', the Precentor says, 'Light up' And then the church is illuminated.

And the bishop processes from the sacristy with two candlesticks, as we have said before, they stand at the right and left of the altar.

When the litany is finished, the bishop says, 'Glory to God in the highest'. Then the apostle is read. 'Alleluia, Give thanks to the Lord' [Ps 118 (119)], tract, 'Praise the Lord, all nations' [Ps 116 (117)]. They do not sing the offertory, or Lamb of God or the communion. They do not carry a light before the gospel book that night, but only incense.

---

1   In the Gelasian Sacramentary there is a prayer provided before the lessons begin (the text
     is given below). The fact that this *Ordo* explicitly dissents from the Sacramentary ironically
     shows how closely the two are linked.
2   In the days of a good classical education (i.e. rhetoric) it would have been unthinkable to
     use a book for saying the prayers in the course of the service. It is good to see traditional
     standards being maintained here.
3   For the text of the blessing see Whitaker. *DBL*, pp 186-7.

The Vigil Service in the Gelasian Sacramentary

The following text gives alternatives to the use of the Papal liturgy, in that it provides for a blessing of the Paschal candle and a set of twelve vigil readings. The blessing of the candle was allowed by Pope Zosimus (417-8) through the 'paroccia' which may apply to local churches around Rome (beyond the *tituli* in the city) but more probably to local dioceses under Roman influence and control.[1] The form of blessing did not in the long run achieve the popularity of the *Exultet* (see below) but the principle of twelve readings (possibly based on the Jerusalem pattern: see *The Day has Come!*, pp 200-206) became the standard pattern in Gallican liturgies which then influenced the later Roman Missal.

Gelasian Sacramentary

HERE FOLLOWS THE ORDER FOR THE BEGINNING
OF THE VIGIL ON HOLY SATURDAY

First of all between the eighth and ninth hour of the day they proceed to the church and enter the sacristy and put on vestments according to custom. A cleric begins the litany and the priest proceeds from the sacristy with the sacred orders. They come before the altar and stand there with heads bowed for as long as is sung Lamb of God, who take away the sins of the world, have mercy. Then the priest rises from prayer, goes behind the altar and sits in his chair. Then the archdeacon comes before the altar and receives the light which was hidden on the Friday. He makes the sign of the cross on the candle and lights it, and he performs the blessing of the candle.

O God, the creator of the world, the author of light, maker of the stars; God who uncovered with clear light the world which lay in darkness; God through whom brightness had a beginning in your ineffable power; we humbly offer to your majesty this candle from your own gift and invoke you in your works on this most holy night-time vigil. The candle is not polluted with the grease from flesh or spoilt with profane unction, or touched with sacrilegious fire, but is put together from wax, oil and papyrus in the honour of your name and lit, and we offer it to you with the obedience of pious devotion. This is a great mystery and marvellous sign of this night which must be heaped with worthy praise. In the miracle of the Lord's resurrection the age-long darkness realized that day had dawned upon it, and death, which once had been condemned to eternal night, was amazed to see the bright light of the coming of the man and to find itself dragged as a captive in the Lord's triumph. What had been condemned through the dark audacity of the first created being's transgression, now shines with the splendour of freedom through the miracle of this night. Coming to the veneration of this feast-day with fervent spirit, as human piety demands, we show to you, our God, peaceful lights with the glow of flames, so that as they melt with full faith, they sing the praises of your creation. For it can be said that it was through the light of the flame that the power of divinity deigned to appear to Moses,

---

1   Per paroccia concessa licentia cereum benedici. Cf. *Fire and Light*, p 306.

and by its saving light it led the people who were leaving the land of slavery. It preserved life with softer blandishments for the three children who had been thrown into the oven by the tyrant's judgement. For just as the horror of darkness is dispelled by the advancing grace of this light, so, O Lord, the burden of sin is destroyed as the light of your majesty shines upon it. And so when we marvel at the beginning of this substance, we must praise the origin of bees. Bees indeed are frugal in their needs, and most chaste in procreation. They build little cells made of liquid wax, quite beyond the learned art of human skill. They collect flowers with their feet and nothing harmful is found in the flowers. Childbirth does not harm them, but they collect with their mouths swarms of new conceived young, just as Christ proceeded from his Father's mouth, a marvellous prototype. Their virginity is fruitful without giving birth, a means which our Lord deigned to follow, and decided to have as his earthly mother with love of virginity. Therefore such gifts are offered to you, O Lord, as worthy of your sacred altars, and Christian devotion is confident of your joy in them.

BLESSING OVER THE LIGHTING.[1] So let the generous pouring of your blessing, almighty God, come upon this flame and this brightness of the night,. Unseen ruler, look on, that not only may the sacrifice which is offered by night shine with the hidden mixture of your light, but in whatever place anything from the mystery of this sanctification is taken the power of your majesty may be present and the wickedness of diabolic fraud be expelled. Through Jesus Christ your Son our Lord, who lives and reigns with you in the unity of the Holy Spirit, God for ever and ever. Amen.

After this the priest rises from his chair and says the prayers of the paschal vigil, as is contained in the sacramentary.

XLIII
PRAYERS FOR EACH OF THE LESSONS ON HOLY SATURDAY

O God, you bestow the riches of your mercy most especially on this night, have mercy on every order of your priestly ministry, and sanctify all the grades of our service with the perfect forgiveness of their sins, so that you may not suffer those who will minister to your regenerating grace to be subject to any offence. Through.

The reading follows: In the beginning God created . . .

O God our constant strength and eternal light, graciously look on the marvellous mystery of your whole Church and in tranquillity perform the work of salvation of mankind by the effect of your perpetual providence, and may the whole world perceive that what it sees is thrown down is now being built up, and what has grown old is being renewed, and all things are returning to wholeness through him from whom they received their origin, through.

---

1 'Lighting' or 'fire' is the original meaning of *incensus*, but with time the change to mean 'incense' caused this part of the prayer to become one for the blessing of incense, separate from the rest of the prayer.

The reading on Noah follows

Almighty and eternal God, you are marvellous in the dispensation of all your works, may your children who have been redeemed understand that greater than the wonder of the creation of the world in the beginning was the sacrifice of Christ our Passover at the end of the age, through the same Lord.

The third, on Abraham

O God, the supreme Father of the faithful, you multiply the children of your promise throughout the world by widespread adoption, and by the sacrament of Easter you made Abraham your servant to be the father of all nations, as you swore, grant that your people may enter into the grace of your calling, through.

The fourth, in Exodus, with the canticle, Let us sing to the Lord

O God, we see the sparkle of your ancient miracles even in this present age when what you conferred on one people in freeing them from persecution by the Egyptians by the power of your right hand, you work in the salvation of the nations through the water of baptism: grant that all the peoples of the world may come to be among the children of Abraham and the dignity of the people of Israel. Through.

The fifth, in Isaiah

Almighty and everlasting God, multiply in honour of your name what you promised to the faith of our forebears, and increase the children of promise by holy adoption, so that what the saints of old did not doubt would happen, your Church may recognize as greatly fulfilled. Through.

The sixth, in Ezekiel

O God, you bid us in the pages of both testaments to celebrate the paschal mystery, grant us to understand your mercies, so that from the reception of present gifts we may have a firm expectation of gifts to come. Through . . .

The seventh, in Exodus

O God, you have made the variety of all the nations to be one in the confession of your name, grant that we may desire and be able to do what you command, so that the people who are called for eternity may have one faith in their minds and one obedience in their actions. Through.

The eighth, in Deuteronomy with the canticle

O God, who raise up the humble and strengthen the righteous, you taught your people through your servant Moses to sing this holy song, so that the repetition of the law would be our guidance: rouse your power for the fulness of the nations who are justified, and grant joy by melting terror so that with your forgiveness wiping out the sins of all, what had been denounced for punishment may pass to salvation. Through.

The tenth in Daniel

Almighty and everlasting God, the only hope of the world, you declared the mysteries of the present age through the song of your prophets, graciously increase the desires of your people, because no increase of virtue comes in any of the faithful except by your inspiration. Through.

Prayer after psalm 41
Almighty and everlasting God, look in your mercy on the devotion of your people who are born again, and who, like the hart, desire the fountain of water, and in your mercy grant that the thirst of their faith may sanctify their body and soul by the mystery of baptism.

Then they process to the baptistery with a litany for the baptism . . . (see *ORR 1*, p.16)

The Exultet

The most famous formula for blessing the paschal candle is the *Exultet*, a somewhat complicated formula. It begins with a preamble in which the deacon asks the congregation for its prayers for him as he sings the main *praefatio* or proclamation, which is introduced by the traditional formula, 'Let us give thanks to the Lord our God: It is right and just'. The florid symbolism of the proclamation owes much to Virgil's description of bees in the *Georgics*, one section of which is quoted for explanation.

The *Exultet* was popular in Gallican areas and so found its way into the 'alternative' form of the Easter vigil included in the Gallican supplement to the Gregorian Sacramentary, and from there it has become the standard form of blessing the paschal candle.

EXULTET: Text: R. Cantalamessa, *La Pasqua nella chiesa antica* (Turin, 1978), reproducing the text of B. Capell,e in Miscellanea G. Mercati 1 (Studi e Testi 121, Città del Vaticano, 1946), pp.225-8.

Now let the angelic host of heaven rejoice, let the divine mysteries rejoice, and let the trumpet of salvation sound for the victory of the great King! Let the earth be glad that she has been lightened by the rays of this great brightness and, illumined by the splendour of the eternal kingdom, let her know that darkness has been dispelled from over the whole world. Let mother Church rejoice in the adornment of the blaze of so great a light, and let this building resound with the full voices of the people.

Therefore, dearly beloved, I pray you who are here present in the marvellous brightness of this holy light, call upon the mercy of almighty God together with me, that he who graciously called me, unworthy as I am, to join the number of his levites, may pour the grace of his light upon me and enable me to celebrate the praise of this candle. Through . . .

It is indeed right and just to praise with the service of our lips and with all our hearts and minds the invisible God, the almighty Father, and his only-begotten Son, Jesus Christ our Lord, who for us paid to the eternal Father the debt of Adam, and by his precious blood wiped away the record of our former sins.

For this is the feast of the Pasch, in which that true Lamb is killed and his blood consecrates the doorposts. This is the night in which first you brought our forebears the children of Israel out of Egypt and made them to cross the Red Sea with dry feet. This is the night which cleansed the darkness of sins by the light of the column of fire. This is the night which now separates from the evils of the world and the shadows of sins all who believe in Christ, restores them to grace and unites them to holiness. This is the night in which the bonds of death are broken, and Christ ascends, victorious from the dead.

For life would be no use to us without the benefit of redemption. O marvellous bestowal of your love towards us! O deepest love past understanding! To redeem a slave, you delivered up your Son. O most necessary sin of Adam, which was wiped out by the death of Christ! O happy fault, which deserved to have such and so great a redeemer! O blessed night, which alone deserved to know the time and hour when Christ rose from the dead. This is the night of which it is written, 'The night shall shine as the day', and, 'The night is my light in my joy'. This night's holiness puts wickedness to flight, washes guilt away and restores innocence to the fallen and joy to those who grieve; it puts hate to flight, makes peace, and bows down earthly powers.

And so, holy Father, in the grace of this night, receive the evening sacrifice of this flame which the all-holy Church renders to you in the offering of this candle, by the hands of your ministers and the work of the bees. We know the meaning of this column which the shining flame lights up in honour of God. Although it is divided and shared, it suffers no diminution of the shared light; it feeds on the melting wax which the mother bee brought forth to form this precious lamp.

The bee surpasses all other animals subject to mankind; of tiny body, it has a great heart beating in the narrow confines of its breast. Puny its strength, mighty its spirit!

Knowing the changes of the seasons, when they have shed the white of frosty winter and removed the icy old age with the softer winds of spring, at once the need comes upon them to go forth to their work. Scattered over the fields, balanced for a moment on their wings, with legs arched, they swoop down to collect in their mouths the flowers of the garden. With provisions loaded up they make their way back to camp. There, some by a wonderful skill are setting up the cells with strong glue, others are assembling their children using their mouths, and others are packing nectar into the young they have collected from the leaves.

O bee truly blessed and wonderful, whose chastity suffers no violence from sexual intercourse nor is bruised by pregnancy nor destroyed by childbirth. O night truly blessed which ravaged the Egyptians and enriched the Hebrews; night when things in heaven are joined to things on earth.

We pray you, Lord, that this candle which we have consecrated in honour of your name may continue to burn without dimming, to dispel the shadows of this night, that it may be accepted by you as an fragrance of sweetness and joined with the lights of heaven. May the morning star meet this flame, the morning star who has come back from the dead and shone with peace on mankind. We therefore pray, Lord, that you will graciously grant a time of peace to us your servants, all your clergy and faithful people, and preserve us in this Paschal time.

Most you shall marvel at this habit peculiar to bees—
That they have no sexual union; their bodies never dissolve
Lax into love, nor bear with pangs of birth their young.
But all by themselves from leaves and sweet herbs they will gather
Their children in their mouths, keep up the queenly succession
And the birth-rate, restore the halls and the realm of wax.
(Virgil, *Georgics*, IV, lines 197-202, trans. C Day Lewis, OUP, Oxford, 1966).

Early History of the Proclamation

The *Exultet* is certainly an early document, and is generally dated to the later fourth century. We know little of the development of the genre of the blessing of the candle, except through a letter of Jerome to the deacon Praesidius, a deacon of Piacenza. From the correspondance we learn that it was traditional for the deacon not only to deliver the *praefatio* but also to compose it. Praesidius was turning to Jerome for help in this respect. Jerome seems to accept the custom as well-known and established, though he dislikes it intensely, and the resulting letter could be the earliest surviving Christian parody of Christian liturgy.

From this and other evidence it seems likely that the tradition of the paschal candle and its blessing originated in North Italy. We have other compositions surviving: two by Ennodius of Pavia, and a few lines of one composed by Augustine of Hippo, in metrical form. Links are generally made in the literature with *lucernarium* lamp-lighting which was part of the Roman liturgy as witnessed in the early third century by the *Apostolic Tradition*, though it must be said that if there is any direct evolution in Rome the link is with the two candles carried in the Papal liturgy. The single wax candle, large like the pair in Rome, seems to have attracted the symbolism of the pillar of fire of Exodus, and the Trinitarian symbolism of the wax, wick and flame is strong in the literature. The curious attraction of Virgil's bees is owed to the tradition that they are meant to reproduce without sexual intercourse, a matter of some interest in an age in which the ascetic life was growing in importance. But it seems that all these features were standard from early on, and served as ready material for the deacon's *praefatio*. The importance of the original composition leads me to include here two *praefationes* by a bishop, Zeno of Verona. He gives no evidence in his sermons of the existence of the deacon's ministry of the paschal proclamation (nor need we expect him to have done), but we see a similar genre of rhetorical composition which was evidently enjoyed and respected by the congregation.

Jerome, *Ep. 18 to Praesidius, PL* 30, 182-8.

Jerome to his brother Praesidius, greeting. 'Nothing', says the comic poet, 'is so easy, that an unwilling spirit cannot make it difficult'. If he thought it was difficult to do something easy with an unwilling mind, what do you think I am able to do in such a very great matter and with no eloquence of exposition? For whoever have wanted to proclaim the praise of the candle and to spread out the sail of their mind, as they say, to the stormy winds, to leave the familiar shore and forge out into the open sea, at once these orators hold the stage with their clamour—a picture of flowers and meadows, words falling softly like the whispering breeze. And bees are pictured, which are born and give birth without intercourse, because they alone are free from sexual union. They gather their children in their mouths, skillfully assemble them and, by some life-giving spirit, instil a soul not from themselves into the infant bees. Besides this the whole of Virgil's Georgics is brought to the fore: the king flying in at the head of his troop, and their various functions are described with such a racket that you would think you were actually in the camp with the army. But when you hear or read this, you will praise the orator's eloquence, and, briefly to mention it, I suppose you will remember Quintilian's exercise, in which the poor man in grief over the death of his bees pleads that the flowers have been poisoned by the furious and intemperate rich man. So suppose that all this is enjoyable and delights the ear with its poetic metre, what has this to do with a deacon, or the mysteries of the Church, or the Paschal season when the lamb is slain and they eat the flesh on the bone with girded loins? Then the bishop is silent and the presbyters are reduced, as it were, to the place of the laity, and the deacon holds forth and teaches what he has scarcely learnt, and by his proclamation on this most solemn occasion, then has a whole year's moratorium imposed on his voice. Do you not see the absurdity of it all? You understand that you are asking a difficult thing, indeed it is the most difficult thing of all, at the same time to write what is to be proclaimed and to teach why the proclamation is of this kind. For I almost forgot that it should be about divine rather than human oracles. Read the Pentateuch, go through the Old Testament. Nowhere is there any use of honey in the sacrifices to God, or of wax. But you will see the lights of lamps and flames fed with oil. Why should I speak of the Old Testament? go through the books of the New. These, unless I am mistaken, are the four Gospels, the Acts of the Apostles, and their epistles, and the Apocalypse of John, nothing beyond that. Is there a wax light anywhere? . . .

Zeno of Verona: the sermons delivered at the paschal vigil
Text: Tractatus, ed. Löfstedt, Corpus Christianorum, Series Latina 22
Translation: G. Jeanes, *The Day has Come!*

I. 6: HERE BEGINS A PROCLAMATION

On its laborious path, proceeding though the daily apportionments of its worldly work in its returning circuitous route and returning by its own tracks from itself to itself, ever new in its life-giving death, the day of salvation has come, lavish with every kind of gifts for all who attend on the Lord's mystery. For it grants pay to loyal priests, to subordinate ministers the advancement of promotion, the fruit of immortality for the baptized (*fideles*), healing for penitents, the way of light for catechumens, for the *competentes* the remission of all their sins, and thus it gathers all into the one grace of the body of Christ and leads them to the heavenly realms through our Lord and saviour Jesus Christ, who is blessed for ever and ever.

II. 19: AGAIN ON THE DAY OF THE PASCH

1. Repeating his tracks in the solemn multiple circuit of the worn mile post, the charioteer of the eternal chariot, the day of salvation has come. The same as its predecessor and as its successor, ever new in its long old age, the parent of the year and the year's offspring, it precedes the seasons which it follows and gives birth to its own beginning from its end so as to sow the ages and bring them together. **2.** This is when, similarly, but once only, out of love for his humanity its maker, our Lord and God, died and rose again (*occidit et exortus est rursum*), never indeed to repeat his death (*occasus*). This, I say, is when the darkness of the dead was plundered, when death was subdued, when hell was forced to pour out alive those people whom it had received dead. God the Father almighty will grant that we may celebrate it with our brothers always and everywhere, increased in faith, numbers and love.

2.
Liturgies of Penance

Any modern consideration of penance would profit by thinking about the practice and assumptions of the public liturgies which were used in the ancient Church. Rome was only one example of this. The basic logic was originally very different from our own outlook. As far as minor sins were concerned, the ancient conscience seems to have been reasonably robust. The daily recitation of the Lord's Prayer included the petition for forgiveness, and that seems to have sufficed both for individuals and for the day-to-day liturgical expression of sin and forgiveness. But major sins were a very different matter. Even from the period of the New Testament there was a difficulty in conceiving how someone who had been baptized and was a temple of the Holy Spirit could commit some serious offence. There was a widespread assumption that by so doing they had virtually negated their baptism, they could no longer be seen as possessing the Spirit or being a member of the community of the Spirit, the Church. God may forgive them in the next world, but it was extremely difficult for the community to negotiate the reconciliation of one who had rejected Christ and the Church by their actions. The modern literature about the period, especially concerning the characters and careers of Tertullian and Cyprian, is immense and beyond the scope of this study. In brief, penance was allowed once, and once only, after baptism. The penitent would be barred from ordinary attendance at church and of course from receiving communion. There would be a place for the penitents (or even several places, for different grades of penitents) within or at the entrance to the church, and they earnestly sought the prayers of the faithful for their reconciliation with God and their eventual readmission into the congregation. Early forms of intercession often included mention of the penitents, and they might receive a special hand-laying and dismissal from the bishop just as the catechumens did. Eventual re-admission was subject to the judgement of the bishop. This might be delegated to a presbyter, but one gains the impression that through the early centuries the pastoral care of penitents would have occupied a large amount of the time and efforts of senior clergy. By and large, notorious sins apart, the pastoral work was private and confidential (Nectarius, bishop of Constantinople, closed down the entire system of penance there for a time in 391 after a breach of confidentiality) but the period of penance and the process of reconciliation were still public. The time varied. In the east it could be extremely brief; in the west it was lengthy and penance could easily be for a number of years (in the earliest period, life-long). Inevitably it shortened as mercy and softness tempered early zeal.

Because of the link with baptism (in effect its recapitulation: re-entry to the community of the saved), the penitential liturgy began to imitate the catechumenate. Penitents had their place and were prayed for like the catechumens. Admission to communion was structured around the Easter celebrations. Zeno of Verona speaks as though the penitents would receive communion for first time at the vigil, whatever form of reconciliation they had undergone earlier (see the chapter on Easter above). In Rome as elsewhere the service of reconciliation was held on the Thursday before Easter. (Not being a fast day, it was a convenient day for getting things ready for Easter, hence the blessing of the oils on that day. The timing of both was entirely utilitarian, and not connected with the idea of it being the day of the Last Supper, a calendrical observance which grew up subsequently.) The service of reconciliation became a major event, evidently with a large congregation fulfilling their role as intercessors for the penitents and active agents in their reconciliation with God and the Church. The bishop and clergy play their part, but together with, not apart from, the laity. The major feature is the address by the archdeacon as the advocate of the penitents to the bishop. Originally this seems to have been a free composition, but a set form is adopted. The bishop reconciles the penitents by a series of prayers. There is no formula of forgiveness or absolution.[1]

What we possess of the penitential liturgy of the Roman church belongs to the sixth to eighth centuries as represented in the collection of the Gelasian Sacramentary. There are, as with the rest of this book, Gallican additions, but much of the material is early Roman. No doubt there are still notorious sinners whose reconciliation is a matter of public concern, but the penitents would have included those who underwent public penance as a matter of personal piety. Even from the fourth century people who felt themselves near death would seek to be enrolled among the penitents and then be reconciled, just as those who had not been baptized would call the priest in emergency. It was always more prudent to seek to do penance for one's sins, however small, in this life, before one came before the judgement seat of Christ. In all likelihood such a penitent would have been advanced in years (penance was still unrepeatable, and the penitent was meant to lead a modest and extremely

---

1 Sozomen describes the whole process of penance and reconciliation in Rome, starting with the rite of admission to the order '. . . where there is a place appropriated to the reception of penitents, in which spot they stand and mourn until the completion of the service, for it is not lawful for them to take part in the mysteries; then they cast themselves, with groans and lamentations, prostrate on the ground. The bishop conducts the ceremony, sheds tears, and prostrates himself in like manner; and all the people burst into tears and groan aloud. Afterwards the bishop rises first from the ground, and raises up the others he offers up prayer on behalf of the penitents and dismisses them. Each of the penitents subjects himself in private to voluntary suffering, either by fastings, by abstaining from the bath or from divers kinds of meats, or by other prescribed means, until a certain period appointed by the bishop. When the time arrives, he is made free from the consequences of his sin, and assembles at the church with the people.' *Historia Ecclesiastica* VII, 16; Dallen, *Reconciling Community*, p 68

disciplined life even after reconciliation[1]) and more a pious than a notorious sinner.

The service of reconciliation was the most public and genuinely celebratory part of the liturgical provision. We are also given prayers for enrolling a new penitent (just as there was a form for making someone a catechumen). This is placed in the sacramentary at the beginning of Lent, and there is also provision for placing the penitent in a place of seclusion, a monastery or such, at this time. The practice is taken seriously but is being ritualized. After the public reconciliation there is provision for reconciliation of a penitent at death (added here as an appendix to the public rite), and finally, the formulae for a mass which concludes the public rite of penance.

BIBLIOGRAPHY
CAP, vol.3, 101-8.
T Talley, 'The Liturgy of Reconciliation' in Worship: Reforming Tradition (Pastoral Press, Washington 1990, 59-74).
J Dallen, The Reconciling Community (Pueblo, Collegeville, Minnesota, 1986).
J A Favazza, The Order of Penitents (Liturgical Press, Collegeville, Minnesota, 1988).
K Rahner, Theological Investigations vol. 15 (ET DLT, London, 1983).

The penitential rites: the Gelasian Sacramentary

XV

PRAYERS AND PRAYERS OVER THE PENITENTS
[*rite for admission to the order of penitents at the beginning of Lent*]

Lord, hear our prayers and spare the sins of those who confess to you, so that your merciful forgiveness may absolve those whom their guilty conscience accuses. Through.

May your mercy come to this your servant, we beseech you, O Lord, and all his iniquities be wiped out with speedy forgiveness.[2] Through our Lord.

Give heed to our prayers, O Lord, and do not let the mercy of your compassion be far from this your servant; heal his wounds and forgive his sins, so that he may not be separated from you by any iniquities but always be able to cleave to you his Lord. Through.

---

1 Pope Siricius (+399): 'Despite having been penitents, like dogs they return to their vomit. Like pigs they wallow in mud. They want to hold public office, to enjoy sports and recreation, to marry and enjoy its pleasures without inhibition. To publicize their lack of self-control they father children despite their vows.' *Ep. 1.5 PL* 13, 1130-31; trans. Dallen, *Reconciling Community*, p 75.

2 'speedy' (*celeris*) refers to a felicitous progress through the discipline of penance. Cf the last prayer of this set. But Dallen, p 69, in his translation reads *celestis*, 'heavenly'.

24

Lord our God, you do not overcome our offence but you are appeased with our satisfaction; look, we beseech you, on this your servant who confesses that he has sinned grievously against you. It is in your power to grant the washing away of crimes and to offer mercy to sinners, for you have said that you prefer the penitence of sinners to their death. Therefore grant this, O Lord, that he may so celebrate the vigils of penitence before you that his behaviour may be corrected and you will grant that he may celebrate eternal joys in your presence. Through.

[*The following prayer is said by Dallen to be a Gallican addition, as is demonstrated by its more picturesque language.*]

Lord, I pray for the pity of your majesty's name, that you will graciously grant pardon to this your servant who confesses his sins and offences, and release him from the debts of his crimes in the past. You brought back the lost sheep on your shoulders to the fold, you were appeased by the tax collector's prayers and confession; be appeased also, O Lord, to this your servant, in your kindness give heed to his prayers, so that as he remains in tearful confession he may speedily beseech your pity and, being restored to your most holy altars, he may be built up again by hope of eternal glory in heaven. Through.

XVI
ORDER FOR THOSE DOING PUBLIC PENANCE

You receive the person on the Wednesday morning at the beginning of Lent[1] (quadragesima) and cover him with a hair shirt, you pray for him and put him in seclusion until the day of the Lord's Supper. On that day he is presented in the body of the church. The bishop says the prayer of reconciliation over him prostrate on the ground on the Thursday of the Lord's Supper, as can be found there.

XXXVIII
PRAYERS ON THE THURSDAY [OF HOLY WEEK]

ORDER FOR THOSE DOING PUBLIC PENANCE

The penitent comes out from the place where he has done penance and is presented in the middle of the church prostrate on the ground. And the deacon makes his request in these words:

The acceptable time has come, O venerable bishop, the day of divine propitiation and of human salvation, on which death received its end and eternal life its beginning, when there is to be a planting of new shoots in the vineyard

---

1 This specific date is important evidence for the growth of the custom of starting Lenten observance on the Wednesday before Quadragesima, the modern Ash Wednesday. These prayers belong in the Sacramentary with prayers for the week between Quinquagesima and Quadragesima, and which include prayers on the Wednesday for the beginning of the fast. (§§ XVII—XVIII)

of the Lord of hosts so as to effect a clearing and healing of the old. For although no season lacks the riches of the goodness and kindness of God, now however sins are forgiven more generously by his mercy and those born again are received more eagerly by his grace. We are enlarged by those who are to be born again; we grow also by those who return to us. The waters wash; and so do tears. On the one hand there is joy at the reception of those called [to baptism]; on the other there is gladness at the forgiveness of penitents. And so it is that your suppliant, after falling into various forms of crimes by neglect of heavenly commandments and by the transgression of his wrong conduct, lies prostrate in humility and cries to God with the words of the prophet and says, 'I have sinned; I have acted wickedly, I have done wrong. Have mercy on me, O Lord', and hears with an attentive ear the words of the gospel, 'Blessed are those who mourn for they shall be comforted'. As it says in scripture, he has eaten the bread of grief, he has soaked his bed with his tears, he has afflicted his heart with mourning and his body with fasting, so that he may recover his soul's health which he had lost. There is one judgement on penitence which is advantageous to each and assists all. And so this person who has been stirred to the performance of penance by such great examples, bears witness before the Church who has lamented over him, O venerable bishop, and says, 'I acknowledge my iniquities and my sin is ever before me. Turn your face from my sins, O Lord, and wipe out all my iniquities. Restore to me the joy of your salvation and strengthen me with the spirit I enjoyed at first.' Since he prays thus and pleads for the mercy of God with a contrite heart, mend in him, apostolic bishop, whatever has been corrupted by the devil's destruction, and by the protective merits of your prayers make the person most close to God through the grace of divine reconciliation; so that he who was formerly displeasing through his lawless behaviour may now rejoice that the author of his death has been defeated and he is pleasing to God in the land of the living. Through our Lord.

After this the bishop or another priest gives warning that he must not return to and repeat what he has washed away in penitence. Then the priest says these prayers over him.

Give heed, O Lord, to our supplications, and kindly hear me who more than anyone need your mercy. You have made me a minister of this work not through a choice based on my merit but through the gift of your grace. Grant that I may be faithful in following your bounty and you yourself in your kindness work through my ministry. Through

Grant, we beseech you, O Lord, to this your servant the worthy fruits of penitence, that by achieving the forgiveness of sins he may be restored unharmed to your holy Church from whose integrity he had deviated in sin. Through our Lord.

O God, the most beneficent founder and most merciful creator of the human race, who by the blood of your only Son redeemed mankind which had been cast down from eternity by the devil's hatred: give life to the one whom you do not wish to die, and receive the one who you could not leave lost but have restored to the right way. We beseech you, Lord, may the tearful sighs of this your servant move your kindness. Heal him of his wounds. Hold out a saving hand to the one who lies before you, lest your church should be robbed of any part of its body or your flock suffer any loss, or the Enemy exult in the damnation of one of your household and the second death possess one who has been reborn in the saving font. To you, therefore, Lord, we pour out our suppliant prayers and the weeping of our hearts. Spare the one who confesses so that he may not be subject to the punishments threatened by the sentence of future judgement. May he not know what terrifies in the darkness, what shrieks in the flames, and may he not return in vain from the way of error to the path of righteousness, only to suffer from new wounds, but may what your grace has conferred and your mercy made again be kept safe for him for ever. Through.

AGAIN FOR THE RECONCILIATION OF A PENITENT

Almighty and eternal God, in your kindness loose the sins of this your servant who confesses to you, that he may no longer be brought to punishment by his guilty conscience but to forgiveness by the mercy of your kindness. Through our Lord.

Almighty and merciful God, you answer swift confession with the forgiveness of sins, come to help the fallen, have mercy on those who confess, and release with the power of your kindness those who are bound by the chains of their offences. Through.

O God, you purify the hearts of those who confess to you and release from every bond of iniquity those whose consciences accuse them, grant forgiveness to the guilty and apply medicine to the wounded, so they may receive the forgiveness of all their sins and henceforth may remain steadfast with sincere devotion, and suffer no loss of eternal salvation. Through

Lord, holy Father, almighty and eternal God, look on this your servant who has been overwhelmed by the hostile storms of the world and condemns his own faults with tearful lamentation. Receive his tears and groans with kindness and call him back from darkness to light. Grant a cure to the one who confesses, wholeness to the penitent, and the help of healing to the wounded. May the Enemy no more have power over his soul: freely accept his confession, purify him and restore him to your church, and bring him into the presence of your altar, so that he may be admitted to the sacrament of reconciliation and may be worthy to give thanks to your holy name together with us. Through.

XXXVIIII
RECONCILIATION OF A PENITENT AT DEATH

Merciful God, compassionate God, according to the multitude of your mercies you wipe out the sins of these who do penance and you cancel the guilt of past offences with the mercy of forgiveness, look on this your servant and when he calls upon you, hear him as he begs for forgiveness for all his sins with a heartfelt confession. Renew in him, most kindly Father, whatever has been corrupted with earthly frailty, or whatever has been violated by diabolic fraud; restore him in the unity of the body of your Church with perfect forgiveness. Have mercy, O Lord, on his groans, have mercy on his tears, and since he has no confidence in anything save your mercy, admit him to the sacrament of reconciliation. Through.

We humbly beseech your majesty, O Lord, that you may graciously grant the mercy of your forgiveness to this your servant who has been defiled by the long squalor of penitence, that he may receive the wedding garment and be counted worthy to come to the royal table from which he had been evicted. Through.

We beseech your majesty, O Lord, holy Father, almighty, eternal God, who continually look not for the death of sinners but their life, look on the weeping of your servant, look kindly on him as he lies prostrate before you, and by your mercy turn his weeping into joy. Tear up the sackcloth of sin and put on him saving joy, that after the long hunger of his wanderings he may be filled from your holy altars, and enter the inner chamber of the royal palace and for ever bless your glorious name. Through our Lord.

Merciful God, compassionate God, you never confine your forgiveness to particular times, but you open the door of your mercy to one who knocks, and you do not abandon penitents even at the very end of this life. Graciously look on this your servant who with a heartfelt confession desires forgiveness of all his sins. Renew in him, most kindly Father, what has been corrupted by diabolic fraud in deed, in work and in thought, and bind in the unity of the body of your Church this limb of your redeeming. Have mercy on his groans, have mercy on his tears, and since he has no confidence in anything save your mercy, admit him to the sacrament of reconciliation, for with you no healing of any soul is difficult or slow while it is yet in this body. For you are faithful in your words, in saying that the sinner should not put off conversion for a long period of time but that he should quickly mourn before you. Through.

PRAYERS AFTER RECONCILIATON OR AFTER
HE HAS RECEIVED COMMUNION

God, you purify the hearts of those who confess to you and free from every bond of iniquity those whose conscience accuse them. Grant forgiveness to the guilty and apply medicine to the wounded, that they may receive remission of all their sins and henceforth remain steadfast in your sacraments with sincere devotion, and suffer no loss of their eternal salvation. Through

After this the people make their offerings, and the sacraments are consecrated.

SECRETA [prayer over the offerings] God of the heavenly powers, from the dew of your grace it comes down that we should have access to your mysteries with purified senses, grant, we beseech you, that as we observe these things handed down to us we may solemnly offer you a pleasing service of praise. Through

INFRA ACTIONEM [Within the prayer] In fellowship with and celebrating the most holy day on which our Lord Jesus Christ was betrayed, and also the memory.

ITEM INFRA [Again within the prayer] We therefore beseech you, O Lord, to look kindly on the offering of your whole family which they offer to you on the fast day of the Lord's Supper on which our Lord Jesus Christ gave to his disciples the mysteries of his body and blood to be celebrated, so that they may be worthy to offer whole and unblemished gifts to you over many years; and that you will order our days in peace . . .

Again within the canon, when we say, On the day before he suffered, *in the celebration of this day we say* Who on this day, before he was betrayed, took bread in his holy hands, lifted etc.

POST COMMUNIONEM [After Communion] Grant, we beseech you, O Lord, that we may know in body and mind the mystery of the new sacrament which we have received.

AD POPULUM [Over the People] Good shepherd, look with kindness on your flock, and do not allow the sheep whom you have redeemed with the precious blood of your Son to be torn by the attacks of the devil. Through our Lord.

3.
Rome and her Neighbours: Baptismal Commentaries

In *ORR 1* I included a translation of John the Deacon's commentary on the baptismal rites, and used it to illustrate the text of the rites in the Gelasian sacramentary. Even allowing for the fact that the liturgical text comes from a later date than the commentary, there is, as I mentioned then, something ill-fitting about John the Deacon's description. In part that is due to misunderstandings about a liturgy which had developed for adult initiation and was now adapted for infants. But he was also using some text as the basis for his commentary, which he refers to as an 'ancient record' (*vetus pagina*). I believe that some other traces of this 'ancient record' have come down to us in the sermons which go under the name of Pseudo Maximus of Turin, but who has been called by Giuseppe Sobrero, his most recent editor, the 'Anonymous of Verona' (after the place where the most important manuscript is found, rather than any necessary link of the author to that city).[1] Eleven sermons have survived, of which three are an incomplete set of commentaries on the baptismal rites. It has long been recognised that there are parallels between the Anonymous and John the Deacon. At first it was believed that the former was dependant on, and therefore to be dated after, the latter. But Sobrero has proposed that in fact John has borrowed from the Anonymous. I take a third path, that both writers are borrowing from a common source. I have two main reasons for this. First, they both refer to other, unnamed, authorities. Just as John mentions the 'ancient record', so the Anonymous invokes the tradition, institutions and the rule (*regula*) of the Catholic Church in a way which would fit with a text which commented on the rites and which commanded respect. The second piece of evidence for my theory of a common source is that the commentary by the Anonymous is incomplete: one sermon which described the anointing of the breast and the renunciations is missing, even in the important Verona manuscript which dates from the late sixth to the early seventh century, and it is most likely that it never entered the public domain with the eleven sermons of the collection. But we have another, later writer, Leidradus of Lyons, who again provides a parallel version of part of the baptismal commentary. His version is very close indeed to that of the Anonymous, while John the Deacon gives a looser rendering. But the description of the anointing of the breast in Leidradus and John show parallels even though that passage is missing in the Anonymous. Therefore it is most likely that Leidradus is using, not the Anonymous (as has been previously thought) but a source common to all three writers.

---

1   *Anonimo Veronese: Omelie Mystagogiche e Catechetiche*, Bibliotheca 'Ephemerides Liturgicae' Subsidia 66 (Rome 1992).

I hope in a later work to explore the nature of these early anonymous commentaries (I suspect they were of a kind of 'living literature' which were being constantly adapted). Suffice it here for us to see that the understanding of the Roman rite even at an early period was affected by her neighbours. John the Deacon, asked to write a commentary of the liturgy of Rome, did the thing we all do and found another commentary on which to base his own work, and imposed its structure on the liturgical practice of Rome. Unfortunately the commentary did not fit. At times John was aware of the fact and actually mentions his discomfort at one point. But elsewhere he may well have been influenced without noticing. He omits the notion of opening in the 'Effeta' rite, he speaks of an anointing with oil rather than spittle as in the Gelasian rite, and he describes only a single post-baptismal anointing whereas the Roman use had long included a double anointing. In all these cases he could be reflecting his source commentary rather than the actual liturgy of his day. It is possible that he was accurate, but the doubt remains.

The text given below is that of the three sermons by the Anonymous, with footnotes including the parallel passages of John the Deacon (already translated in full in *ORR 1*). Then the most important section of Leidradus is added, showing the parallels with the Anonymous and with John.

The Anonymous of Verona: Sermons 5-7 (On Baptism 1-3)

V. CONCERNING THE ANOINTING BY THE PRIESTS OF THE NEOPHYTES' EARS AND NOSTRILS WITH HOLY OIL

Every godly address, dearly beloved brethren, ought to be heard with all attention and diligence of the mind, but especially this one which we will today address to your Charity. And so, now the catechumens have been dismissed, we have kept you back in order to hear this, since in addition to those things which it is right for all Christians to observe in common, we shall be speaking specifically about the heavenly mysteries which only they who receive them by our Lord's grace can hear. Therefore you must hear what we are saying with a greater reverence since they are committed only to the baptized and the faithful,[1] and are more important than those which even catechumens are able to hear.

You must not be surprised, dearly beloved brethren, that we have said nothing to you about the mysteries during the mysteries themselves, that we did not give the interpretation at the time of their administration, not indeed because of negligence (that would be sacrilege in such holy and divine matters) but out of piety. For we ascribe to such holy and divine matters the honour of silence, and among the holy splendour of the mysteries we refrain from the business of teaching, so that we may venerate more by our silence the majesty of the divine grace which cannot be properly explained by any human speech.

---

1   *fideles*, signifying those who have been baptized on an earlier occasion.

But since it is necessary for you, my friends, to be instructed and taught everything, now the rite of the mysteries has been completed, we are explaining to you what earlier we have conferred on you, lest you might think that the dignity of the divine mystery is less precious because you do not understand it. If you have understood it, you will see everything which is believed to be precious in this world is most worthless compared with so great a sacrament. And so let each of you carefully note the form of each of the mysteries which, by God's grace, you received through our ministry, and now carefully understand those things which then you received in innocence and faith, so that you may be able to serve your understanding all the better.

First[1] of all we anointed your ears with the oil of blessing, but hear the reason why it is done by all the catholic priests of Christ according to the tradition of the Church. *Faith[2] and all heavenly teaching gains its entry to the spirit through the ears, and from hearing comes understanding. No one can recognise the sacraments of faith, unless he hear the preacher, as the blessed apostle asserts when he says, 'How* shall you hear without a preacher', and again, And so *faith comes from hearing, and hearing through the word of God'. And so it is right that the organs of sense are sanctified by that oil, and faith cannot come to the spirit without it, and at the same time people will come to baptism so as to keep their ears undefiled by any evil or base word* to their lives' end, and like deaf people may not hear anyone speaking ill of their neighbour or any obscene or immodest talk. Thus they fulfil the saying in holy scripture which says, *'Fence in your ears with thorns and do not hear a wicked tongue'. And elsewhere, 'Do not believe the vain things you hear'*, and *again, 'Give your heart to discipline and prepare your ear to words of prudence'.*

And so the holy anointing which is applied to *the ears signifies that they should avoid and flee all undisciplined speech as contradicting Christian teaching, and turn only to hear the words of God, because,* having been anointed by that oil, *they should consecrate their hearing to the words of Christ.* For he speaks to the Father through the prophet and rejoices in the obedience of the people who believes in him when he says, 'You did not desire sacrifice and offering, but you have perfected ears for me'. Then indeed the ears of the faithful are perfected for Christ, when they desire to hear nothing but Christ and the things which belong to Christ. The Lord was speaking of this in the gospel when he was talking about the mystery of the kingdom of heaven, 'Whoever has ears to hear, let him hear'.

While it is ordinary nature to have ears, it is not ordinary to have 'ears to hear'. For whoever spurns the words of God, although they cannot spurn them unless they have previously heard them, nevertheless they can be said not to

---

1 Cf. John the Deacon (*Studi e Testi* 59 (1933), 158-79): Their ears are touched with the oil of sanctification, and so are their nostrils. Their ears are touched for the reason that faith enters through them for understanding, as the Apostle says, 'Faith comes through hearing, and hearing through the word of God', so the ears are as it were fortified by a kind of wall of sanctification, so that they cannot admit anything which might be harmful or lead them back. (*ORR 1*, pp 15-16.)

2 The italicized passage is to be found also in Leidradus (see below).

have heard them in that they have spurned what they heard—they despise what they have heard as though they had never heard it. And so they have ears, which can be said to be not 'ears to hear' but ears of disobedience. As I might say, they hear only in order not to hear, that is, so that what they hear they reject as though, as we have said, they never heard it. Only those who firmly commit to their spirit what they hear with their ears, and what they have committed to their spirit they follow in action, are said by Christ to have 'ears to hear'

The Lord speaks about hearers of this kind in the gospel, 'Blessed are your eyes which see and your ears which hear'. And again, 'Everyone who hears these words of mine and does them, will be like a wise man who built his house on a rock, and the rain came down and the floods rose, and the winds came and blew upon that house, and it did not fall, because it was founded upon the rock'. Again about those who hear badly, who have ears but they are ears of disobedience, he affirms, 'Everyone who hears my words and does not do them, is like a foolish man who built his house on sand, and the rain came and the floods rose and the winds blew, and they all fell upon that house and it collapsed, and great was its ruin'.

So you see what a difference there is between the one who hears well and the one who hears badly, that is between the one to keeps the words of God and the one who, when he hears them, rejects them as though he had never heard them. To him who obeys and does them, it is wisdom; to him who rejects them, it is foolishness. The former builds his foundation on solid rock; the latter's construction is unsound and, without foundation, is described as easily collapsible. The first has stability; the last has ruin—and the ruin is total. No one is more utterly ruined than the one who has heard the word of God and turns to the sins on account of which 'eternal punishments have been prepared'. But you, after your ears have been anointed with blessed oil, have been placed in the company of the wise hearers, and having rightly heard the words of God, that is, fulfilling what you hear, may you hear Christ saying to you on the day of judgement, 'Come, you who are blessed by my Father, receive the kingdom which has been prepared for you from the foundation of the world'.

But[1] do not think that the performance of the mystery, that we anointed *your nostrils* with the oil of blessing, was pointless or lacking in purpose. It can be understood to have been done *so that[2] those who come to baptism are admonished*

---

1 Cf. John the Deacon: When their nostrils are touched, no doubt they are admonished to remain steadfast in the service and commandments of God for as long as they draw the breath of life through their nostrils, as the holy man said, 'As God lives, who has taken away my judgement, and the almighty who has brought my soul to bitterness, as long as life is in me and the spirit of God in my nostrils, my lips shall not speak iniquity, nor shall my tongue utter a lie'. There is another meaning in the anointing of the nostrils, that, because the oil is blessed in the Saviour's name, they are led to his spiritual fragrance by some ineffable sweetness of the inner sense, so that in delight they may sing, 'My name is poured out like ointment; we run after the fragrance of your ointments'. (*ORR 1*, p 16)

2 Again the words in italics are to be found in Leidradus.

to keep the sacrament of such a great mystery inviolate and whole even to death, so that they must not desert the worship and service of Christ our Lord God for as long as they draw the breath of this life through their nostrils, as the holy man Job says, 'As God lives who has taken away my judgement, the almighty who has brought my soul to bitterness, as long as breath is in me and the spirit of God in my nostrils, my lips shall not speak iniquity, nor shall my tongue utter a lie. Far be it from me that I should judge you to be just. Until I die, I shall not let go of my innocence, and I shall not abandon my justification which once I laid hold of'.

But a more subtle understanding is signified in this anointing *of the nostrils. For the fragrance of the oil which is blessed in the name and power of Christ draws you to the spiritual fragrance, so that you may be able to perceive Christ by the inestimable sweetness not of the bodily but mental senses,* and with delight in the knowledge of his fragrance and following in his footsteps, you may be able to *say* the words of the chorus of those who believe in the Lord, '*We run after you to the fragrance of your ointments'. The apostle commends this fragrance to Christians when he says,* '*Thanks be to God, who gives us the triumph in Christ Jesus, and manifests the fragrance of knowledge of him through us in every place, because we are the sweet fragrance of Christ to God'.*

Think how much the apostles accomplished in perceiving the fragrance of Christ, both in eagerness of preaching and in holiness of life, setting it before all else. As they spread the sweet-scented fragrance of Christ everywhere, they themselves became a sweet fragrance to God. We would wish, dearly beloved brethren, that this is fulfilled in you too, so that as you receive the sweet fragrance of the knowledge of Christ, *a most delightful fragrance may ascend before God from the holiness of* your *lives.* Through Jesus Christ our Lord, who lives and reigns with the Father and the Holy Spirit.

VI. ON THE MYSTERY AND HOLINESS OF BAPTISM

In the first sermon we promised that we would speak about everything that you received through our ministry and the grace of Christ, lest any negligence should arise in you out of ignorance. But we had a care for your difficulty and did not then say everything to you at once. We paid attention to your understanding and memory, and we took care that your mind should not be tired of listening and fail to understand everything nor should your memory be weighed down with the consideration of so many things all at once and quickly omit and lose even what it had understood.

So in the first and second sermons[1] we only spoke to you about those things which we conferred on you in accordance with the tradition of the Catholic rule before you came to the holy baptistery: we explained what the anointing signified and what the various meanings are of the anointing of the various

---

1   The second sermon, which the Anonymous will shortly summarize as covering the renunciation of the devil and probably the anointing of the breast, is missing from this series.

parts of your body as our Lord deigned to grant, and we showed how you were prepared through the oil of sanctification to hear the full faith and you were called to the 'sweet fragrance of Christ', and ordered to 'renounce the devil' from the bottom of your heart. Now we will speak about the deeper mysteries which are celebrated in the holy baptistery itself.

You gave a most solemn guarantee in which you promised to renounce 'all his pomps and works and all devilish fornication', and you went down into the font: the holy font, the font of life, the font of redemption, the font sanctified with heavenly power, and sanctified so as to sanctify people by washing them after many sins.

For you must not regard those waters with bodily eyes, but with spiritual sight. For, while the substance of the water is of the common nature of all waters, its specific effect comes from the grace and power of God who made water to wash away the bodily and visible filth. And so he sanctified water through which he would wash away invisible sins by the hidden power of his might. For the Holy Spirit works in that water so that those who are guilty of various crimes before baptism and sentenced to burn with the devil in the hell of eternal fire might be held worthy after baptism to enter the kingdom of heaven. Thus the Lord expresses the might of this great sacrament in the gospel when he says, 'Unless one is born again of water and the Holy Spirit, one cannot enter the kingdom of God'.

So before we baptized your whole body in this font, we asked, 'Do you believe in God the Father Almighty?' You replied, 'I believe'. And again we asked, 'Do you believe in Christ Jesus his Son, who was born of the Holy Spirit and the Virgin Mary?' Each of you replied, 'I believe.' Again we asked, 'And in the Holy Spirit?' Likewise you replied, 'I believe'. We did this according to the command of our Lord and Saviour Jesus Christ, who when he ascended to his Father in heaven gave this command to his disciples, that is to the apostles, 'Go and baptize all nations in the name of the Father and of the Son and of the Holy Spirit and teach them to observe all that I have commanded you'.

Let no one who hears of the Father and Son and Holy Spirit imagine that we confess three gods. May that sacrilege be far removed from our faith. We acknowledge that there is one God, as he himself affirms, 'I am God, and there is none else besides me, there is no righteous one or saviour besides me. Turn to me and be saved, for from the ends of the earth I am God and there is none besides me'. And in another book, 'Hear, O Israel, the Lord your God, the Lord is one'. And again, 'The Lord your God is in heaven above and on the earth beneath, and there is none besides him'.

So we hold to and believe in three persons, that is the Father and the Son and the Holy Spirit, of one power, one substance, one eternity, one will, one godhead, and we revere the whole Trinity and call upon one God. It is a pagan sacrilege to believe in many gods, and again it is heretical madness not to believe in three persons of one substance in one godhead, equality and coeternity. We have quoted Christ's clear authority for this: 'Baptize all nations in the name of the Father and of the Son and of the Holy Spirit'.

But when we asked, 'Do you believe in the holy Church and the forgiveness of sins and the resurrection of the flesh?' we did not ask so as to mean, that one believes in the Church of God in the same way as one believes in God. For the holy and catholic Church is holy and catholic precisely because it has a right belief in God. So we did not say that you should believe in the Church in the same way as you believe in God, but you are to understand that we were and are saying that as you pass your life in the holy and catholic Church you believe in God, and also you believe in the coming resurrection of the flesh.

So just as you have believed in the mystery of the Trinity, and you have received one God in the name of the Father and of the Son and of the Holy Spirit, just as you have believed that your sins are to be forgiven and now through baptism you believe they have been forgiven, so you believe in the coming resurrection of the flesh, something you indeed promised to believe in.

For the whole Christian hope consists of this things, that we believe that in truth the resurrection will be of this body and of no other, and just as we stand now in the church before the altar of God, so we believe that on the day of judgement we shall stand before the judgement seat of God, as blessed Paul the apostle says, 'You must all appear before the judgement seat of Christ, so that everyone may receive according to what he has done in his body, whether good or bad'. That is what unbelieving souls do not believe will happen.

And there are some who promise with their lips to believe, but in their heart they have no hope, and thus give great offence to almighty God by believing that he cannot raise and give life to people after their death. But we who hang our faith on the words of God cannot doubt our resurrection. For we believe that since God created human beings who formerly did not exist, he can easily promise to refashion those who have already existed. He made heaven and earth and the sea and all that is in them, and all the elements, how can he not be able to make again the people whom he once made with the intention that they should be judged in another life for actions done in this one, and deserve either rewards for good deeds or punishment for evil?

This is the faith of catholic Christians that we believe that we shall rise with the soul which we have now and in the body with which we are now clothed, and we have a fitting example of the resurrection in Christ himself, our Lord, the Word of the Father. Although he is God and the Son of God, the Word of God and in his divine nature co-eternal and co-equal and consubstantial with the Father, yet he took our human nature in which he was ready to be born of a virgin, and afterwards suffer and die, and on the third day he rose again and ascended in heaven, so that he might fire in us the hope of resurrection. And we believe that we shall be raised from the dead in the same way as we confess Christ rose from the dead. As the apostle says when he attacks those without faith, 'If Christ is preached as having risen from the dead, how can some of you say that there is no resurrection of the dead?'

So hold to this firmly and believe what is proclaimed by God's word, that there will be a resurrection in which a glorious immortality will be given to all the saints who love Christ and do his will, so that they will rejoice for ever in the sight of God with the angels and the heavenly powers. But the faithless and sinners and those who do not obey God's commands will rise only for their flesh, now made immortal to be condemned to eternal flames so that it will burn for ever and find no respite from the flames. The word of our Lord Jesus Christ testifies to this when in the gospel he said about sinners, 'Then they will go away to eternal punishment, but the righteous will go to eternal life'.

So after you had promised to believe those things which we have explained so far, we immersed your heads three times in the sacred font. The[1] rite of baptism which we celebrate signifies a twofold mystery. You were rightly immersed three times, since you received baptism in the name of the Trinity; you were rightly immersed three times, since you received baptism in the name of Jesus Christ who rose from the dead on the third day. The threefold repeated immersion reflects the pattern of the Lord's burial, through which you have been buried with Christ in baptism and been raised with Christ in faith, so that your sins may be washed away and you may live in holiness by imitating Christ and his merits, as the apostle says, 'Do you not know, that as many of us as have been baptized in Christ Jesus have been baptized in his death? We have been buried with him through baptism into his death, so that just as Christ rose from the dead through the glory of the Father, so we also should walk in newness of life. For if we have been planted with him in the likeness of his death, so we shall also share in his resurrection. We know that our old self was crucified with him, so that the body of sin might be destroyed and we may be slaves to sin no longer'.

Consider, dearly beloved brethren, the condition of the baptised as described by the apostle: he says, 'that we may be slaves to sin no longer'. To receive forgiveness of your sins through baptism and then be ready to be bound up in sin again; to have been made holy after being a sinner, and willingly to turn from saint to sinner again; and to return to the filth of sins after the holy font which can only wash you clean once, is that not utter, I shall not say negligence, but rather madness?

So take care, dearly beloved, that you keep whole and unstained what you have received to your life's end, since you can never receive it again. Now that you are once and for all made sinless, always keep clear of all sins. Christ in his mercy cleansed you from your filth and the dirt of the devil's ways, and now you are clean he does not wish you to be made filthy again. To him be glory ith the Father and the Holy Spirit for ever and ever. Amen.

---

1 Cf John the Deacon: In this mystery the baptism is performed by a threefold immersion, and rightly so. For whoever comes to be baptized in the name of the Trinity must signify that Trinity by threefold immersion, and acknowledge that he is indebted to the kindness of the one who rose for him on the third day from the dead. (*ORR 1*, p 17)

ON THE ANOINTING OF THE HEAD AND THE FOOT WASHING

So far we have spoken about the mysteries which are celebrated either before the sacrament of baptism or at the baptism itself. Now we shall deal with those which by holy tradition are performed on the newly baptized.

When the baptism has been completed, we pour chrism, that is the oil of sanctification, on your head.[1] By this oil it is shown that the Lord confers on the newly baptised the dignity of royalty and priesthood. In the Old Testament those who were chosen for kingship or the priesthood were anointed with holy oil, and they received power from the Lord by the anointing of the head, some to rule the people of God, others to offer sacrifices to God. Thus we read that holy David and others were anointed kings by prophets and from private citizens were changed by the sanctification of the oil into kings. And we read that holy Aaron was anointed by Moses and from being a lay person was consecrated by the holy oil as a priest of the Lord. Thus it is said in the psalm 'As the ointment on the head, which flows down on the beard, even the beard of Aaron'. But in the Old Testament that oil conferred a temporary kingdom and a temporary priesthood which were to be exercised in this life and ended after the span of a few years. But this chrism, that is, this anointing which was administered to you, conferred on you the full riches of the kingdom and priesthood of Christ, and once conferred it is never brought to an end.

Perhaps you are surprised that we said that you have obtained by this chrism the priesthood and kingship of the glory to come. It is not I who declare that this dignity is conferred on you, but the apostle Paul, indeed through the apostle Christ himself. For he speaks in this way to the 'faithful', that is to those who have been washed in baptism and consecrated with chrism: 'You are a royal and priestly nation, a holy race, God's own people, so that you may proclaim the power of him who called you out of darkness into his marvellous light'.

So consider the honour which you have obtained in this mystery, and take care that, now you have been made children of the kingdom through baptism after the sins you had earlier committed, you should not desire to return to your sins (God forbid!) and become children of hell. For can you imagine God's anger if you should wish to return to your sinful behaviour after his benefits and the forgiveness of your sins, and after your adoption as children of God, if you should wish to reject God again as though you were slaves and do the devil's will?

---

1   Cf John the Deacon: Then they put on white garments, and the head is anointed with the unction of the sacred chrism, so that the newly baptized may understand that in himself a kingdom and a priestly mystery have come together. For priests and princes were anointed with the oil of chrism, the ones to offer sacrifices to God, the others to rule over their peoples. (*ORR 1*, p 18) Although the Anonymous seems to omit any mention of the white garment, it may well have been included in his liturgy since the reference to 'keep whole and unstained what you have received' at the end of the previous sermon is reminiscent of formulae for the white garment; e.g. the *Missale Gothicum*, ed. L C Mohlberg (Rome 1961): 'Receive the white garment; may you bear it unstained before the judgement seat of our Lord Jesus Christ. Amen'.

Now with the completion of all the sacraments, we also gave a command to you by example and word, for we washed the feet of each one of you, to stir you to imitate us, or rather our Lord and Saviour himself. Just as we wash your feet, so you must wash the feet of your brethren and strangers,[1] so that we may teach you not only to be hospitable, but also hospitable with humility, and so to honour those whom you receive in your hospitality that you may not blush to fulfil the task of slaves towards them.

If anyone should find this insulting, and is so puffed up with devilish pride as to refuse to fulfil the Lord's command, and, being noble according to this age, should blush to wash the feet of some poor Christian who is contemptible in this world's eyes, he makes Christ to blush, who both ordered this service and fulfilled it himself—indeed he graciously did it before he gave the command, and set an example in order to give the order more easily. For we read this in the gospel about the Lord Jesus, 'knowing that the Father had given all things into his hands, and that he came from God and was going to God, he rose from dinner and took off his clothes, and tied a linen cloth around him. Then he poured water into a bowl and began to wash his disciples' feet and to dry them with the cloth which he wore about him'. And again, 'After he had washed their feet, he put on his clothes, and when he had taken his place again, he said to them, "Do you know what I was doing for you? You call me master and lord, and rightly so, for so I am. If I, your lord and master, washed your feet, how much more should you wash one another's feet. I have given you an example, that you should do as I have done for you. Truly truly I say to you, the servant is not greater than his master, nor is the apostle greater than the one who sent him. If you know this, blessed are you if you do it".' Consider, then, brethren, how wretched and mad it would be for a servant to refuse to wash a fellow servant's feet, or a disciple the feet of a fellow disciple, after the Lord and master of all did not refuse to wash the feet of his disciples and servants. He humbled himself before his inferiors, but we refuse to humble ourselves before our equals and often our betters. This can only come from a lack of belief in what is to come. For if we truly and with our whole heart believed that we would come to eternal and heavenly rewards through these commands of our Lord which we must keep only for the time of our brief lives, we would not blush to fulfil all the works of humility, we would positively glory in them!

The sermon concludes with a lengthy exhortation to obey God's commands in more than lip service.

---

1   Cf the *Missale Gothicum*: I wash your feet. As the Lord Jesus Christ did for his disciples, so may you do for strangers and travellers, so that you may have eternal life.

Leidradus of Lyons to Charlemagne, 'On the Sacrament of Baptism' PL 99, 857-8.

CHAPTER II

(The italicized words show parallels with the Anonymous of Verona, and those in capitals, with John the Deacon. It will be seen that the link with the latter extends consistently through passages whether or not they are included in the former's surviving text.)

Faith and all heavenly teaching gains its entry to the spirit through the ears, and from hearing comes understanding. No one can recognize the sacraments of faith, unless he hear the preacher, as the blessed APOSTLE asserts when he says, 'FAITH COMES FROM HEARING, AND HEARING THROUGH THE WORD OF GOD'. And so it is right that the organs of sense are sanctified by the oil, and faith cannot reach the spirit without it. It should be realised that there are different practices of this rite in different regions. Some touch the ears and nostrils of the catechumens with holy oil, others with spittle, others again with spittle and oil; also some touch the mouth with oil, following our Lord's example. As it is written in the gospel about the deaf-mute, 'He placed his fingers in his ears'. But whether it is with the touch of oil or some other practice, *their ears* are sanctified, so that *people will come to baptism so as to keep their ears undefiled by any evil or base word* as it is written, *'Fence in your ears with thorns and do not hear a wicked tongue'. And again, 'Give your heart to discipline and prepare your ear to words of prudence'. And so* the holy anointing which is applied to the *ears signifies that* the faithful *should avoid and flee all undisciplined speech as contradicting Christian teaching, and turn only to hear the words of God, because they should consecrate their hearing to the words of Christ.*

The *NOSTRILS also are sanctified likewise with a TOUCH, so that those who come to baptism are ADMONISHED to keep the sacrament of such a great mystery inviolate and whole even to death, so that they must not desert the worship and service of Christ our Lord God for AS LONG AS THEY DRAW THE BREATH OF THIS LIFE THROUGH THEIR NOSTRILS, AS THE HOLY MAN Job SAYS, 'AS GOD LIVES WHO HAS TAKEN AWAY MY JUDGEMENT, THE ALMIGHTY WHO HAS BROUGHT MY SOUL TO BITTERNESS, AS LONG AS BREATH IS IN ME AND THE SPIRIT OF GOD IN MY NOSTRILS, MY LIPS SHALL NOT SPEAK INIQUITY, NOR SHALL MY TONGUE UTTER A LIE'. But a more subtle understanding IS SIGNIFIED in this sanctification OF THE NOSTRILS. For the touch DRAWS the faithful to the SPIRITUAL fragrance, so that you may be able to perceive Christ by the inestimable sweetness not of the bodily but mental senses, and say, 'WE RUN after you TO THE FRAGRANCE OF YOUR OINTMENTS'. The apostle commends this fragrance to Christians when he says, 'Thanks be to God, who gives us the triumph in Christ Jesus, and manifests the fragrance of knowledge of him through us in every place, because we are the sweet fragrance of Christ to God'. Therefore the faithful should live in* such a way that *a most delightful fragrance may ascend before God from the holiness of* their *lives.*

The catechumens ARE also now ANOINTED ON THE BREAST and between the shoulders with exorcised OIL, when they renounce Satan and his works and pomps. We think this is done so that THE HABITATION OF THE HEART is signed in front and behind, and the DEVIL, the author of perfidy, is repelled by the sign, and CHRIST the giver of faith and love enters in. For the person's heart is the SEAT of error and sins when it is possessed by the devil, and it is made the habitation of faith, hope and love when it is defended and illumined by Christ. As it is written, 'From the heart come evil thoughts, adultery, fornication, murder'. And, 'You shall love the Lord your God with all your heart'. Therefore the hearts of the catechumens are rightly anointed at the renunciation of the devil, so that he might leave them along with all his works and pomps.

THE GROUP FOR RENEWAL OF WORSHIP (GROW)

This group, originally founded in 1961, has for over twenty-five years taken responsibility for the Grove Books publications on liturgy and worship. Its membership and broad aims reflect a highly reforming, pastoral and mission-ary interest in worship. Beginning with a youthful evangelical Anglican mem-bership in the early 1970s, the Group has not only probed adventurously into the future of Anglican worship, but has also with growing sureness of touch taken its place in promoting weighty scholarship. Thus the list of 'Grove Litur-gical Studies' on page 44 shows how, over a twelve-year period, the quarterly Studies added steadily to the material available to students of patristic, refor-mation and modern scholarly issues in liturgy. In 1986 the Group was ap-proached by the Alcuin Club Committee with a view to publishing the new series of Joint Liturgical Studies, and this series is, at the time of writing, in its twelfth year of publication, sustaining the programme with three Studies each year.

Between the old Grove Liturgical Studies and the new Joint Liturgical Stud-ies there is a large provision of both English language texts and other theologi-cal works on the patristic era. A detailed consolidated list is available from the publishers.

Since the early 1970s the Group has had Colin Buchanan as chairman and Trevor Lloyd as vice-chairman.

THE ALCUIN CLUB

The Alcuin Club exists to promote the study of Christian liturgy in general, and in particular the liturgies of the Anglican Communion. Since its founda-tion in 1897 it has published over 130 books and pamphlets. Members of the Club receive some publications of the current year free and others at a reduced rate.

Information concerning the annual subscription, applications for member-ship and lists of publications is obtainable from the Treasurer, The Revd. T. R. Barker, The Parsonage, 8 Church Street, Spalding, Lincs. PE11 2 PB. (Tel. 01775 722675).

The Alcuin Club has a three-year arrangement with the Liturgical Press, Collegeville, whereby the old tradition of an annual Alcuin Club major schol-arly study has been restored. The first title under this arrangement was pub-lished in early 1993: Alastair McGregor, *Fire and Light: The Symbolism of Fire and Light in the Holy Week Services*. The second was Martin Dudley, *The Collect in Anglican Liturgy*; the third is Gordon Jeanes, *The Day has Come! Easter and Bap-tism in Zeno of Verona*; the fourth is Christopher Irvine (ed.), *They Shaped our Worship*.

The Joint Liturgical Studies were reduced to three per annum from 1992, and the Alcuin Club subscription now includes the annual publication (as above) and the three Joint Liturgical Studies. The full list of Joint Liturgical Studies is printed opposite. All titles but nos. 4 and 16 are in print.

Alcuin/GROW Joint Liturgical Studies

All cost £3.95 (US $8) in 1998—no. 4 and 16 are out of print

1. **(LS 49) Daily and Weekly Worship—from Jewish to Christian**
   by Roger Beckwith, Warden of Latimer House, Oxford
2. **(LS 50) The Canons of Hippolytus**
   edited by Paul Bradshaw, Professor of Liturgics, University of Notre Dame.
3. **(LS 51) Modern Anglican Ordination Rites** edited by Colin Buchanan, then Bishop of Aston
4. **(LS 52) Models of Liturgical Theology**
   by James Empereur, of the Jesuit School of Theology, Berkeley
5. **(LS 53) A Kingdom of Priests: Liturgical Formation of the Laity: The Brixen Essays**
   edited by Thomas Talley, Professor of Liturgics, General Theological Seminary, New York
6. **(LS 54) The Bishop in Liturgy: an Anglican Study**
   edited by Colin Buchanan, then Bishop of Aston
7. **(LS 55) Inculturation: the Eucharist in Africa** by Phillip Tovey
8. **(LS 56) Essays in Early Eastern Initiation** edited by Paul Bradshaw,
9. **(LS 57) The Liturgy of the Church in Jerusalem** by John Baldovin
10. **(LS 58) Adult Initiation** edited by Donald Withey
11. **(LS 59) 'The Missing Oblation': The Contents of the Early Antiochene Anaphora**
    by John Fenwick
12. **(LS 60) Calvin and Bullinger on the Lord's Supper** by Paul Rorem
13-14 **(LS 61) The Liturgical Portions of the Apostolic Constitutions: A Text for Students**
    edited by W. Jardine Grisbrooke (This double-size volume costs double price (i.e. £7.90))
15 **(LS 62) Liturgical Inculturation in the Anglican Communion** edited by David Holeton
16. **(LS 63) Cremation Today and Tomorrow** by Douglas Davies, University of Nottingham
17. **(LS 64) The Preaching Service—The Glory of the Methodists** by Adrian Burdon
18. **(LS 65) Irenaeus of Lyon on Baptism and Eucharist**
    edited with Introduction, Translation and Commentary by David Power, Washington D.C.
19. **(LS 66) Testamentum Domini**
    edited by Grant Sperry-White, Department of Theology, Notre Dame
20. **(LS 67) The Origins of the Roman Rite**
    edited by Gordon Jeanes, then Lecturer in Liturgy, University of Durham
21. **The Anglican Eucharist in New Zealand 1814-1989**
    by Bosco Peters, Christchurch, New Zealand
22-23 **Foundations of Christian Music: The Music of Pre-Constantinian Christianity**
    by Edward Foley, Capuchin Franciscan, Chicago (second double-sized volume at £7.90)
24. **Liturgical Presidency** by Paul James
25. **The Sacramentary of Sarapion of Thmuis: A Text for Students**
    edited by Ric Lennard-Barrett, West Australia
26. **Communion Outside the Eucharist** by Phillip Tovey, Banbury, Oxon
27. **Revising the Eucharist: Groundwork for the Anglican Communion** edited by David Holeton
28. **Anglican Liturgical Inculturation in Africa** edited by David Gitari, Bishop of Kirinyaga, Kenya
29-30. **On Baptismal Fonts: Ancient and Modern**
    by Anita Stauffer, Lutheran World Federation, Geneva (Double-sized volume at £7.90)
31. **The Comparative Liturgy of Anton Baumstark** by Fritz West
32. **Worship and Evangelism in Pre-Christendom** by Alan Kreider
33. **Liturgy in Early Christian Egypt** by Maxwell E. Johnson
34. **Welcoming the Baptized** by Timothy Turner
35. **Daily Prayer in the Reformed Tradition: An Initial Survey** by Diane Karay Tripp
36. **The Ritual Kiss in Early Christian Worship** by Edward Phillips
37. **'After the Primitive Christians': The Eighteenth-century Anglican Eucharist in its
    Architectural Setting** by Peter Doll
38. **Coronations Past, Present and Future** edited by Paul Bradshaw
39. **Anglican Orders and Ordinations** edited by David Holeton
40. **The Liturgy of St James as presently used** edited by Phillip Tovey
41. **Anglican Missals** by Mark Dalby
42. **The Origins of the Roman Rite vol 2** edited by Gordon Jeanes

Grove Liturgical Studies

This series began in March 1975, and was published quarterly until 1986. Each title has 32 or 40 pages. No's 1, 3-6, 9, 10, 16, 30, 33, 36, 44 and 46 are out of print. Asterisked numbers have been reprinted. Prices in 1998. £2.75.